Can You ?

by Cathy French

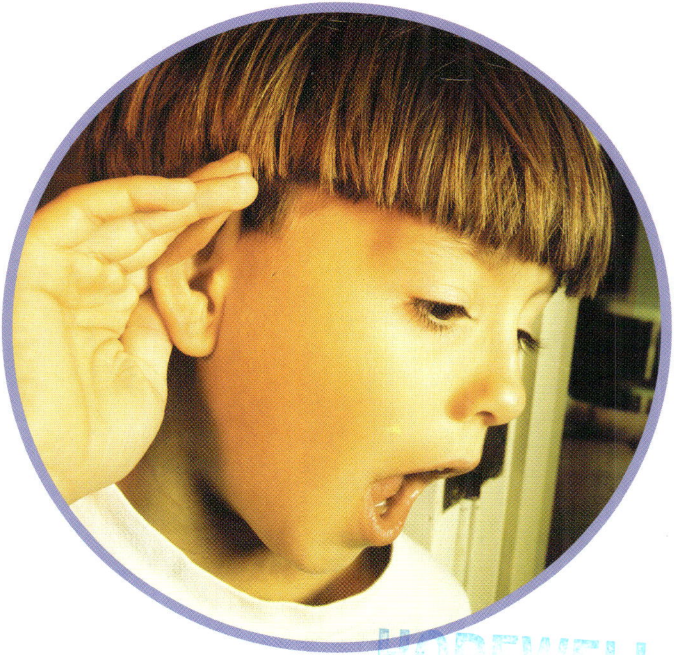

Can you 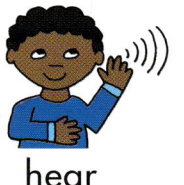 hear
the 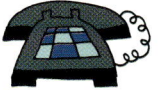 ?
telephone

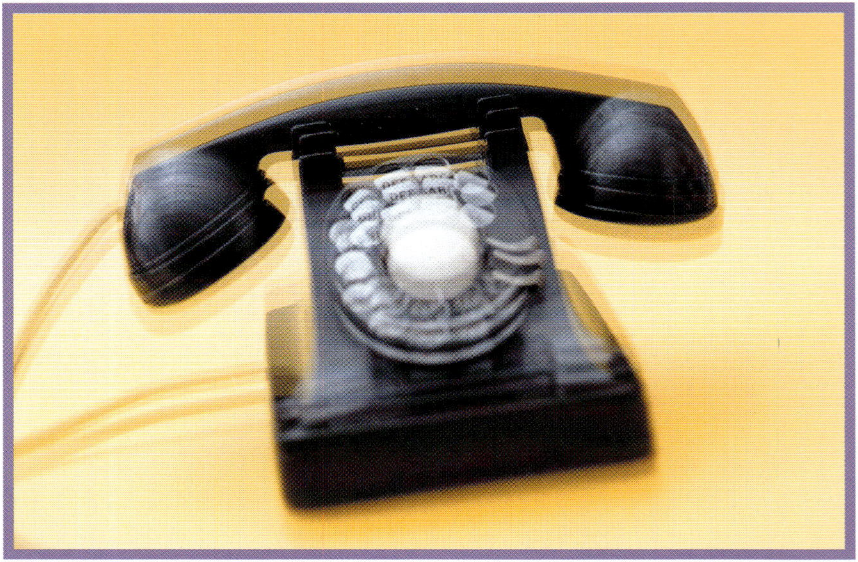

Can you hear the 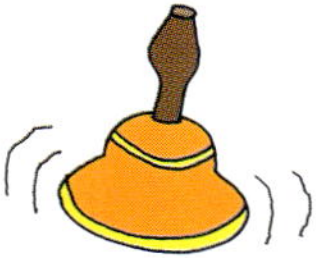 bell?

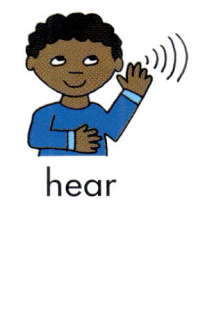

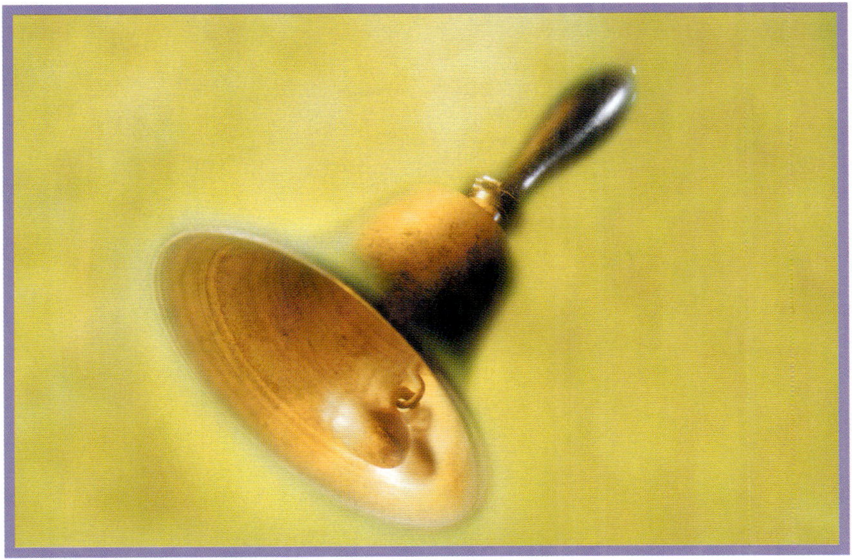

Can you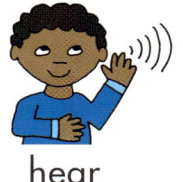
hear
the ?
horn

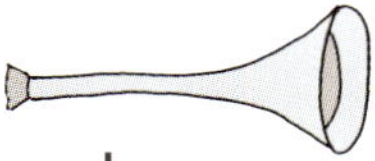

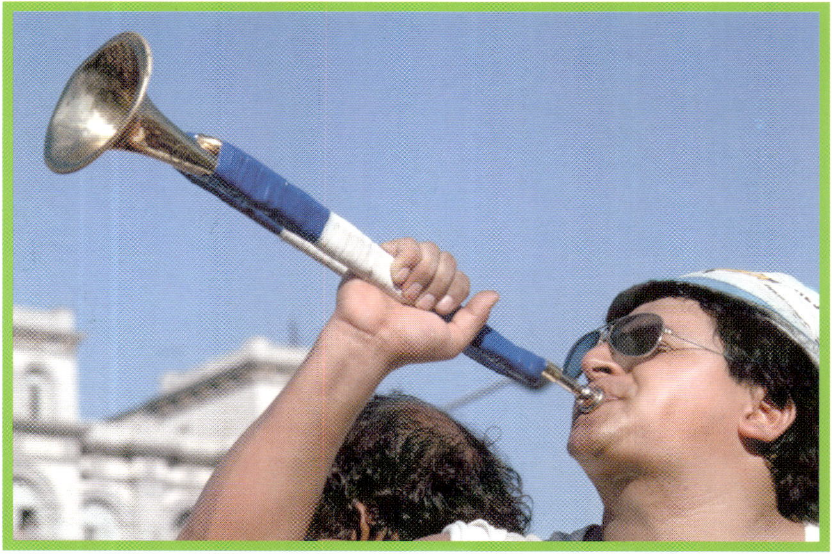

Can you 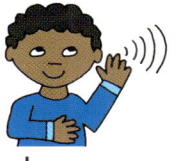 hear
the 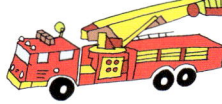 ?
fire truck

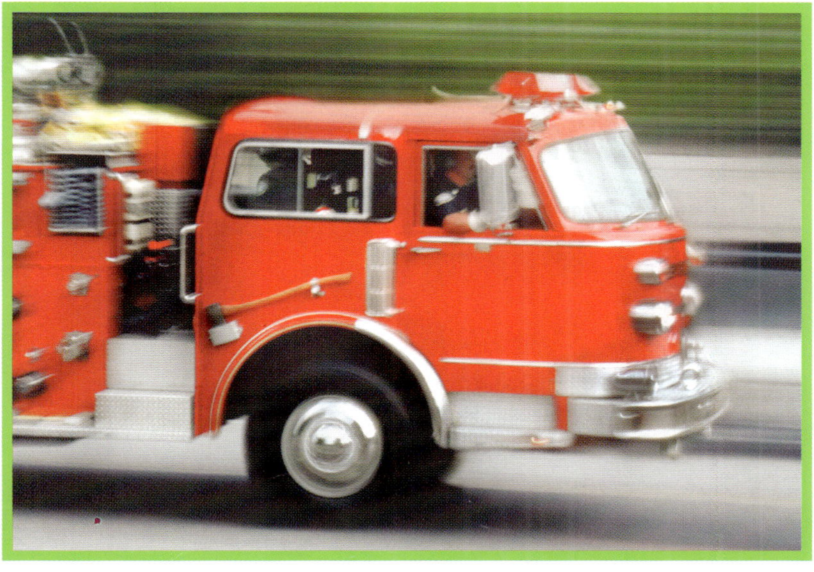

Can you 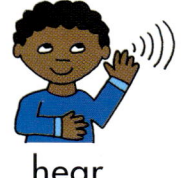 hear the 🚂 train?

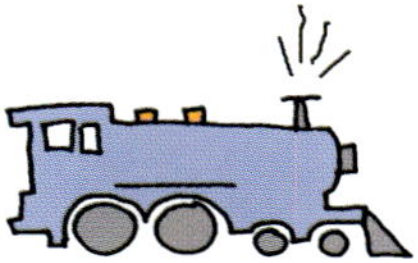

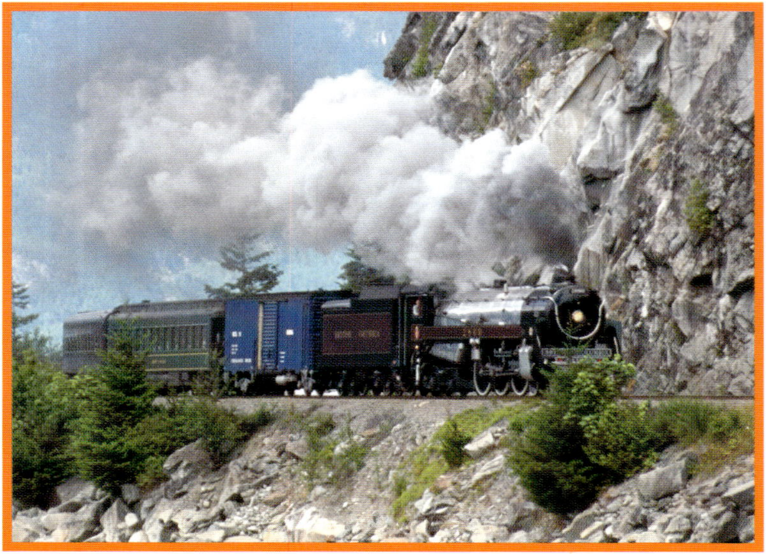

Can you 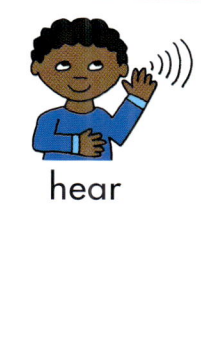 hear the 🐕 ?
dog

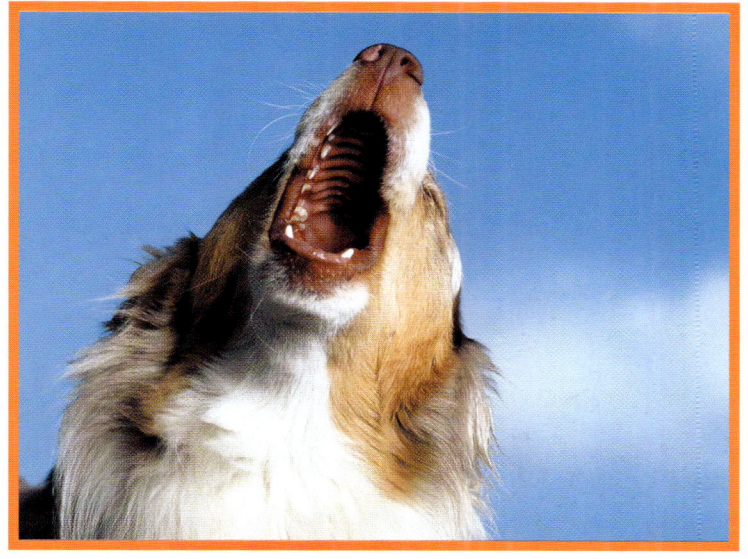

Can you hear the drum?

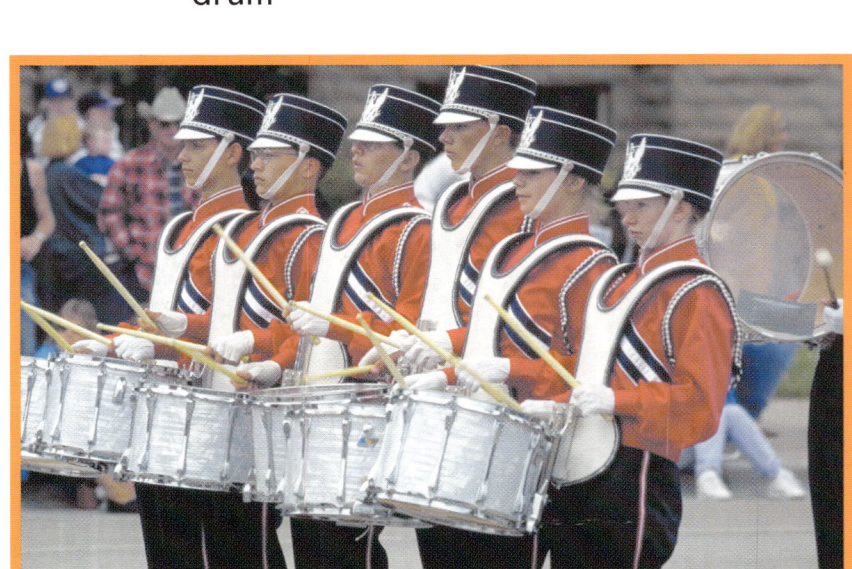